NETWORKING TIDBITS

25 Ways To Connect, Grow & Succeed Through Networking

Ely Delaney

Copyright © 2015 Ely Delaney

No part of this publication may be reproduced or transmitted in any form or by any means, mechanical or electronic, including photocopying and recording, or by any information storage and retrieval system, without permission in writing from author or publisher (except by a reviewer, who may quote brief passages and/or show brief video clips in review).

Disclaimer: The Publisher and the Author make no representations or warranties with respect to the accuracy or completeness of the contents of this work and specifically disclaim all warranties, including without limitation warranties of warranties of fitness for a particular purpose. No warranty may be created or extended by sales or promotional materials. The advice and strategies contained herein may not be suitable for every situation. Neither the Publisher nor the Author shall be liable for damages arising herefrom. The fact that an organization or website is referred to in this work as a citation and/or a potential source of further information does not mean that the Author or the Publisher endorses the information the organization or website may provide or recommendations it may make. Further, readers should be aware that internet websites listed in this work may have changed or disappeared between when this work was written and when it is read.

There is no guarantee, express or implied, that you will earn any money using the techniques and ideas in this book. Examples in these materials are not to be interpreted as a promise or guarantee of earnings. Earning potential is entirely dependent on the efforts and skills of the person applying all or part of the concepts, ideas and strategies contained herein.

Neither the publisher not the author shall be liable for any loss of profit or any other commercial damages, including but not limited to special, incidental, consequential, or other damages.

All of the networking tips in this book have been successful in some businesses, and our intention is that you will be encouraged and inspired to try them in your business. We do not represent that all of the networking tips will work in your business, but that they have been proven to work given the right circumstances. Because we cannot know you or your business, we make no warranty about how they will work for you.

For general information on our other products and services, please find our contact information online at http://YourMarketingUniversity.com

To purchase customized versions of this book or bulk copies of this book, please visit us online at http://YMUBooks.com/booksinbulk

Printed in the United States of America.

Cover Photo - © Can Stock Photo Inc. / matteobragaglio

Cover Design Adapted From Design by Jayson Bailey (http://CookWheelWright.com)

ISBN-13: 978-1500735357 | ISBN-10: 1500735353

ALSO BY ELY DELANEY

Marketing Tidbits: 50 Quick & Easy Ways To Grow Your Business

SPECIAL THANK YOU GIFT FOR YOU!

I believe in good karma!

As a thank you for investing in this book, I want to gift you a copy of my Networking Follow Up Blueprint

Turn Those Stacks Of Business Cards And Connections Into Raving Fans, Eager Followers & Paying Clients

We've all heard that the fortune is in the follow up. Yet most sales are given up on after the 3rd try.

Did you know that most sales are actually made after 6 "touches" with a prospect.

In short, you're giving up too soon!

This guide will show you how to create an immediate follow up system that will turn casual conversations into raving fans and cash paying customers!

Claim your copy of the audio book today at:
http://ymubooks.com/blueprint

In addition to your Networking Follow Up Blueprint, we'll give you even more exclusive marketing tips, tricks and resources that we love to share to help you grow your business and become the Rockstar in your industry!

Go now and get instant access to download your copy of the Networking Follow Up Blueprint immediately!
http://ymubooks.com/blueprint

WHAT PEOPLE ARE SAYING...

"I thought there was a lot of value delivered for the minimal investment. Anyone serious about gaining that slight edge for your business would benefit..." ~Paul Guerrero~

"This was very helpful and informative and provided more specific information than I could find on the internet." ~Michele McClure~

"Ely and Cindy manage and provide excellent content. You won't be disappointed." ~Rick Mueller~

"...gave me information beyond what I expected. Very informative." ~Michelle Maria~

"...filled with usable, effective content. It's a perfect learning experience for small business ..." ~Donnita Parker~

"There is so much really useful content that is broken town in terms we can understand and work with effectively. ...really promotes productivity...." ~Adriana Masser~

"...shows you the key questions you need to answer, and the tools to use (many are free!) that will have the most impact on your bottom line the fastest...This one's a winner." ~Gabrielle Fontaine~

NETWORKING TIDBITS

25 Ways To Connect, Grow & Succeed Through Networking

Ely Delaney

TABLE OF CONTENTS

Also By Ely Delaney 3

Special Thank You Gift For You! 4

What People Are Saying… 5

Table of Contents 8

Networking Tidbit #1 11

Networking Tidbit #2 15

Networking Tidbit #3 19

Networking Tidbit #4 23

Networking Tidbit #5 27

Networking Tidbit #6 31

Networking Tidbit #7 35

Networking Tidbit #8 39

Networking Tidbit #9 43

Networking Tidbit #10 47

Networking Tidbits #11 51

Networking Tidbits #12 55

Networking Tidbits #13 59

Networking Tidbits #14: 63

Networking Tidbits #15 67

Networking Tidbits #16 71

Networking Tidbits #17 75

Networking Tidbits #18 79

Networking Tidbits #19: 83

Networking Tidbits #20: 87

Networking Tidbits #21 91

Networking Tidbits #22 95

Networking Tidbits #23 99

Networking Tidbits #24 103

Networking Tidbits #25 107

Resources 109

ABOUT THE AUTHOR 110

Connect With Ely Online 111

ABOUT MARKETING TIDBITS 112

Networking Tidbit #1

"Every Event You Attend Should Have A Goal"

NETWORKING TIDBIT #1
EVERY EVENT YOU ATTEND SHOULD HAVE A GOAL

Are you attending business events? Chamber meetings, business mixers, even seminars and conferences are all great ways to network and meet new business contacts.

So how do you know it was a success?

Most people network to grow their business and build relationships but they walk in the door just seeing how many they can tell about their amazing product.

I can't count the number of times I've talked to someone that has been going to the same event month after month and feel they haven't got anything out of it.

Why is that?

I believe it's because <u>they didn't have a clear goal</u> as to why they were even at the event.

"To get more business" isn't specific enough (Which is what I hear all the time).

It's about having a very specific goal in mind as to why you're there and what you plan to get out of it.

For me, when I attend an event, I want to meet 2-3 possible leverage partners. People who also serve the same prospect I do and who we can possibly do some cross promotion with. That's usually my number one goal for going to an event.

Think about it. If you know exactly what you're looking for it's a whole lot easier to find it, right? You need to be very specific with who you're looking for and why you're there.

By planning your goal before you even step foot in the event you're much more likely to actually find the right people and can even ask others "Who do you know?" to get introduced to those right people.

Also remember, it's not likely you'll do business right there. People aren't at an event to buy stuff. That's why they go to the mall, not a business mixer.

That doesn't mean it can't happen. Just keep in mind that if you're there pushing your products first, you're likely to scare people off.

Keep it focused on them and how you can get to know them first.

Networking is to meet them. **Then** follow up after the event to build the relationship and see if they are a good prospect for you.

That's when you can tell them more and really get into a deeper conversation.

Another great thing about knowing the goal of attending an event is to know if it's the right place for you. I can't count how many times I see people networking at events because they "should be" but they really aren't in the right place.

If your prospects aren't in the room, why are you there? By prospects, I do mean leverage partners as well. If you lost your keys in the living room of your house you wouldn't check the garage would you?

Again, by having your goal in mind first, you can look objectively at the event you are planning on going to and see if it's the right place for you to be.

Remember, time is valuable and your time may be better spent at a different event or networking online instead. That 3 hours you spend at a business mixer might be better spent following up with your clients and asking for referrals or planning your next workshop.

Action Steps:
- Look at the next event on your calendar
- What's your goal for going?
- Are the right people going to be there?
- Show up with your radar on looking for those people!

Networking Tidbit #2

"Wearing A Name Badge At Events Will Help People Remember You"

NETWORKING TIDBIT #2
WEARING A NAME BADGE AT EVENTS WILL HELP PEOPLE REMEMBER YOU

We all hate the "my name is..." tags they give us at events. But, they actually do make a difference to the people you meet.

Whether you're networking at a conference or your local chamber group, by having a name badge on you're making it much easier for the people you meet to remember you.

It's not uncommon to meet a dozen people at a single event. It's loud and people are talking 100 miles a minute. For me personally, it's not uncommon for me to forget someone's name after 5 minutes of conversation. I'll remember what they do and that I really liked talking to them but I happen to not be so great with names.

In fact, there was a guy I had known for about a year in the networking circles around town. We always had amazing conversations and I really loved chatting with him and catching up but for some reason I just couldn't remember his name.

Finally, at one event he had a name tag on. That was the catalyst that made me remember his name from then on. Many of us are visual people. If we hear it we have a hard time remembering it but if we see it we can remember it for years.

Your name tag is one of those things. By wearing a name tag, you might be helping them solidify your name in their brain.

That brings me to another great reason to wear a nametag. There are people I've met a few times and again, I can't remember their name. They walk up to me and start talking like we're old friends. I feel bad, because I just can't remember the name. I might remember what they do, where I met them and even the last conversation we had but their name just didn't stick with me.

It's a pretty awkward moment and I feel really bad about it. I've personally been there many times. By having a name badge on I can easily glance down and remember their name.

Remember, I'm not the only one like this. In fact, many people have this problem. By wearing a name badge, you're able to help them remember your name without feeling embarrassed to talk to them.

Make it as easy as possible for others. Remember the harder you make it for someone else, the less of an impression you'll make on them.

Spending $10 on a good badge that you can wear at all the events you attend can easily make you much more memorable and the people you meet will appreciate it!

Ely Delaney

Networking Tidbit #3

"The Fortune Is In The Follow Up And It Starts With One Simple Email"

NETWORKING TIDBIT #3
THE FORTUNE IS IN THE FOLLOW UP AND IT STARTS WITH ONE SIMPLE EMAIL

"The Fortune is in the Follow Up"

That's a phrase we hear all the time. It's almost a staple catch-phrase of business culture. Yet, most follow up campaigns fail.

Most of the time it's not because of a poor system. It's simply because there is no follow up at all.

When you're a networker like me, you spend a lot of time driving to events, spending time and energy connecting with other people at the event and paying for the event, parking, food, etc.

You may go to a free event but it still costs a lot to be there. Why not make the most of the time, energy and money spent for each and every event you go to?

The best place to start is with a simple follow up email. We're not talking about anything complicated here. Just a "great to meet you" email.

Before I go into the specifics of making this work and be effective for you, let's talk about a few things that you should never do first.

Rule #1 - Never pitch someone your product via email after you just met them at an event. You've got to build the relationship first. I can't count the number of times I've had someone immediately try to sell their product and tell me how awesome it is.

They tell me how much I need it when they forgot to ask one simple question first... am I even remotely interested in it?

Rule #2 - Don't add someone to your generic newsletter until they say they want it. Just because I gave you my business card doesn't mean I want your newsletter. That's a quick way to get reported as a spammer. I can't count the number of Real Estate Agents who send me their latest listings every week starting about a week after I met them. Even though I never said I was in the market for a new home or to sell mine.

Follow those two rules and you're off to a great start.

So what's the right way to use email to follow up with someone you just met?

Send them an email telling them it was great meeting them at the event. Add value by sharing a few other events they might find useful.

Remember it's about building a relationship and adding value first.

Ask questions about them before telling them about you. Get to know them and show you are interested in them. Then, open up the conversation to chat in person or over the phone. It's setting up an appointment to get to know them more.

Remember they still haven't said they are interested in your products so don't show up with flipchart in hand. (yes I have had that one a couple of times!)

Get to know them first. Then, if it's a fit you can move to sharing more about your products but take it easy. Only do this after you've got to know them and see if they are a good fit for your products first. This is something you can't figure out in 5 minutes at a live event but you can after 30 minutes over coffee.

Simply sending a simple email letting them know you appreciate talking to them and asking for a coffee meeting to get to know them will get you further than anything else.

When you do this right you'll be seen as someone who really cares and is looking to help others. Your reputation will reflect this and people will be lining up to find out more about you.

Networking Tidbit #4

"Want To Meet More People? Greet Them As They Come Through The Door."

NETWORKING TIDBIT #4
WANT TO MEET MORE PEOPLE WHILE NETWORKING?

I've been networking for over 18 years. We all know, many times, it's not what you know but who you know. Or... more importantly, who knows you.

The biggest problem most people have is how to leave a lasting impression on the people who they meet.

One of the best things I have learned and taken action on is to become a greeter.

So what's a greeter?

A greeter is the person who stands by the door and welcomes people as they come in the room. They are the first person people meet as they show up for an event.

Remember back to the first event you attended. You were most likely pretty scared. It's a scary process to walk into a room with a bunch of strangers and try to make new friends. I know when I first started, I was terrified. I didn't know anyone and as a natural introvert, I didn't know what to do.

I do remember a couple of events where someone was standing by the door as I walked in and they introduced themselves to me and to others in the group.

That made it a lot easier.

It's a trait I picked up early on and I've tried to practice it as much as I can ever since. For years, I remembered them and how they took me under their wing to help me out.

Now I'm the one who takes people under my wing to make them feel as comfortable as possible. It's the easiest way to meet new people and get to know them up front. Plus, if you can show you care about someone as they come in the door, you're going to leave a lasting impression.

Even in events I've run I always try to stay near the door. I know there will always be a newbie walking in the door and chances are, they feel like I did at my first few events.

I've also been known to stand outside the door at events I attend just to meet people as they are showing up. I'll introduce myself to them and see if there's someone I can introduce them to.

It's such an easy process yet so powerful. You can be the first person they meet. If you take it to the next level and introduce them to a few other people as well, they will love you for it.

You'll become the one person who really stood out for them and helped them make the most of the event.

THAT will leave a lasting impression with them.

Networking Tidbit #5

"Like A Boy Scout, Be Prepared and Carry Business Cards With You At All Times."

NETWORKING TIDBIT #5
LIKE A BOY SCOUT, BE PREPARED

"I'd love to know more. Do you have a business card?"

I can't count the number of times I've heard that question from people I meet.

Now, as someone who's always looking to network and meet people, I'm meeting people all over the place. Everything from local chamber events to conferences to standing in line at the local coffee shop.

I've actually *done business in the drive-thru of Starbucks* before.

What really amazes me though, is how many people don't bring enough (or any) business cards with them. Like a Boy Scout, you should be prepared at all times. You never know when someone will want to learn more about your business and what you can do to help them out.

Your business card is the most cost effective form of marketing you can do and it's such a simple marketing piece that you can carry with you everywhere.

If you're planning on going to an event to network, make sure you bring 2-3 times the number of cards you think you'll need. You never know what could happen.

I went to an event once where the speaker brought me up on stage to share about my business. At the next break I got swamped and handed out every card I had in my card holder.

Which brings me to my next point... <u>Carry an extra stash with you.</u>

Luckily, at that event I had another stash of cards in my bag I could grab quickly. Without those extra cards I'd have missed out on an opportunity to share with some of those people. Not to mention I had 2 more days of the event.

I keep a stack in my business card holder which is with me all the times, another stack in my bag, which is with me most of the time, another in a bag I keep in my car and even another stack in my jacket pocket.

Altogether, it's not uncommon for me to have 100 cards available just in case.

And yes... there have been times when I've needed every one of those cards.

Even if you're going to the grocery store or hanging out at your kid's baseball game, you never know when a conversation will strike up and you'll have someone asking "Do you have a business card?".

Networking Tidbit #6

"The Wallflower Doesn't Get The Sale"

NETWORKING TIDBIT #6
THE WALLFLOWER DOESN'T GET THE SALE

I'm an introvert by nature. I am perfectly comfortable sitting in a corner and just people watching most of the time.

Though it's pretty entertaining, if you want to get more sales and connect with potential clients and referral partners, then you need to stand up and talk to more people.

Growing up, most of us were taught to talk only when spoken to and to not talk to strangers. That's great when we're 10 and worried about "stranger danger" but when you're in the business world, you've got to get yourself out there and not be afraid to start a conversation with a complete stranger.

Have you ever been at a business event and met two people who sell the same basic thing? I'm sure you have. I've even been in rooms where there's 5-6 people selling the same type of thing. Networking marketing, insurance sales, real estate, financial planning, etc.

It's not uncommon for us to meet several people in any of these industries at any given event.

What makes one stand out more than the next? They all sell the same basic services and products, right?

What makes you want to do business with one over another?

Usually, it's their personality. Most of the time, the one who stands out, gets in front of more people and talks, maybe they share a tip with the group, etc.

No matter what it is they are doing, it's the one who gets up and shares that makes the biggest impression.

If you just stand there and don't talk to people or are the quiet one, you're not giving the impression of confidence in your products and services.

Let's face it, you may be better than them. You might have more training or been in business twice as long as them, but if they stand out more and really shine in front of people, they are more likely to get more people asking them questions and wanting to know more.

Now, for those of you who are shouting... "But that's not me. People should come to me because I have so many more years of experience!"

Guess what... No one knows that.

I know a guy that's in insurance who's been in business for many (and I do mean MANY MANY) years. Yet, he doesn't give me the feeling of confidence he actually knows what he's doing. He's kind of negative and most of the time he's a pretty quiet guy.

When compared to others in the same room every week but come up talking about the latest and greatest things available, he just doesn't shine and I honestly don't feel comfortable trusting him to do the best job for me.

Now, I'm not talking about having to be a professional speaker and getting in front of hundreds of people to give a presentation. I'm talking about stepping up in a crowd of 5 people and talking to them. Share your thoughts and knowledge with them.

Don't be afraid of them. They are in the same boat as you and the best thing is chances are they don't know 10% as much as you about your given craft.

The next time you find yourself being quiet and hiding in a corner at an event, go find one new person you don't know and introduce yourself to them.

You never know, they just might be your next client!

Networking Tidbit #7

"Sometimes The Best Way To Get A Raving Fan Isn't About Your Own Business. It's About Connecting Them With Someone Else."

NETWORKING TIDBIT #7
SOMETIMES IT'S ABOUT CONNECTING THEM WITH SOMEONE ELSE

There's no doubt that we're in business to get more sales. We all need sales to stay in business. That's a given, but sometimes the best way to connect to a person isn't about your business at all.

My favorite questions to ask is, "*How can I help you?*"

It still amazes me how many people are shocked when they hear that question from me. If they have a need for what I offer, then we can continue that conversation. The sad part is if they don't see a need for MY services, then they discount the question completely and can't think of anything.

My favorite part of the conversation, however, is if someone talks about a need that doesn't have anything to do with my business at all and I can still help them.

Maybe they are opening up a new office and need an electrician. They are shocked when I bring up someone I know and offer to introduce them.

I do this all the time. Just last month, I met a woman who does some of the same type of work as another friend of mine.

I immediately said they should connect and as soon as I could I sent an email to both of them introducing them to each other.

She was very grateful. The entire conversation was about how I could help her. Though I couldn't help her with anything related to our products I was still able to help, add value to her, and was happy to make the connection for her.

I have someone else I just met with yesterday and in our conversation I mentioned a plugin we use on our sites. She loved the idea of it and was excited I offered to send her the link to find out more about it.

Neither of those examples took much of my time at all. Yet, both made a huge impression on them and will leave a lasting impression about me being helpful.

When the time arises where either of them need something I have to offer, they will no doubt come back to me. If they meet someone who does need what I offer, I'm sure they will think of me.

It's about being helpful and adding value. Even if it's not about your products and services all the time.

It's the quickest way I know to create an army of raving fans and make a lasting impression on anyone you meet.

Ely Delaney

Networking Tidbit #8

"When You're Networking, Think Like A Farmer, Not A Hunter.

Think Long Term."

NETWORKING TIDBIT #8
WHEN YOU'RE NETWORKING, THINK LIKE A FARMER, NOT A HUNTER

I remember when I first started networking in my local business community. Every group and meeting was different. I had one group where it took six months to actually get my first bit of business.

So many times, I see someone show up at a meeting or two and then they move on to another group. They are thinking like the hunter, expecting an immediate sale from the people they meet.

There's no "courting" phase with them. If they don't get someone to buy within a couple of times attending, they say it's a waste of their time and move on.

Remember, business is about relationships and it takes some work to get people to trust you. In today's fly-by-night world, it takes a lot more to build the trust people need to convince them to hand over their hard earned cash.

You can't expect people to trust you immediately, no matter how great or ethical you are. Remember, they don't know that after once or twice seeing you at an event. It takes time.

Most sales are made between 6 and 12 "touches" with a prospect. That's the norm in today's skeptical society.

You've got to stick it out and show them you're there for the long haul. Showing up a couple of times then disappearing won't cut it.

That's where the farmer mindset comes in. If you walk in to an event with the thought that you're there to cultivate long term relationships that will pay off dividends in the future, it makes life a lot easier for you. First off, it's a lot less pressure than thinking you have to close a sale right then and there.

The farmer knows by spending time taking care of the crops he will get more than enough to cover all his needs in the future. This is how relationship marketing works. It's not about "Who will I sell something to?". It's more of "How can I make a difference in someone's life today?", knowing it will come back 10x in the future.

People buy from the KLT Factor - Know, Like & Trust. That takes time. Especially if they aren't already looking for what you have to offer already.

When someone is already looking to buy what you have, then it's a much easier sale. When you walk into a room and they don't know you, they aren't likely looking for your products. They have other things on their mind (like selling their own stuff).

Take the time to get to know people first. Get to know what's important to them. What needs do they have and is there anything you can do to help solve those needs.

That helps build KLT. Be helpful first and focus on building the relationship so they know who you are and what you do but most importantly, that you're a great person who loves to help. When they are ready to look for someone in your industry, they will think of you first.

That's when the sales start to come in easy and you'll see more business than you can handle.

Networking Tidbit #9

"Conferences & Seminars Are For More Than Just Learning. Sometimes You'll Get More From The People You Meet Than The People On Stage."

NETWORKING TIDBIT #9
CONFERENCES & SEMINARS ARE FOR MORE THAN JUST LEARNING

"Conferences & seminars are for more than just learning. Sometimes you'll get more from the people you meet in the audience than the people on stage."

Conferences are one of, if not my favorite place to network. You can meet more amazing people at a weekend event than you would all month if you know how to do it right.

When attending any conference or seminar, I look at it like any other business event. I walk in the door with a plan to meet specific people.

Spend some time before the event thinking about the type of people you'd like to meet at the event. Are they potential clients, referral partners or even mastermind members?

Who are you looking to meet at the event?
When I walk in the door I have a number in mind of how many people I want to meet who fit a certain profile. That way I know what to look for.

I'm starting conversations and listening to people talk specifically to see if they fit my criteria.

Now more than ever, events encourage networking and want people to connect.

They also want people to help promote the event so they will encourage people to Tweet and post on Facebook about the event. This is one of the best ways to "stalk" people before the event happens.

Check out what people are saying, search social sites for others mentioning the event and reach out to them before the event. Friend them on Facebook and follow them on Twitter.

Comment on a few of their posts and send them a message telling them you'd love to meet up with them at the event and maybe have coffee or something.

This is great if it's your first time and you don't know anyone there. You can make a few friends before you get there so when you show up at the event you'll feel like longtime friends.

Once you're there, seating is often first come, first serve. Try to show up early so you get first pick of your spot at the event.

Even more so, try to get there early so you can find a new spot every day.

Don't try sit in the same spot every day. By moving around the room you get a better chance of meeting new people every day.

This is the quickest way to get to know a bigger crowd during the event and make the most of the event.

Remember, just like local business networking, if you sit with the same people each and every day you never expand your network. You never know if your next client is sitting at the table next to you.

Plan on after hours events

Many times, the after-hours events (AKA drinks after the day's events) is where the real magic happens. I can't count how many huge joint ventures I've seen happen after the main event activities are over with.

I've done business at lunches and met some of the best people hanging out in the bar after the day's festivities. That's where people really connect and get to know each other.

Note: Even if you're not much of a partier, that's ok. Go anyway. I don't drink, yet I've made more friends and great connections just by grabbing a glass of water and being part of the conversation.

Conferences give you a totally different set of people to meet than the norm. I meet a lot of people and it opens up connections with amazing people from all over the world.

I can't find a better place to find a great mix of potential clients, potential leverage partners and great mastermind friends all in one place.

Networking Tidbit #10

"Any Opportunity To Get In Front Of An Audience Is An Opportunity To Share Your Message"

NETWORKING TIDBIT #10
DON'T BE AFRAID OF THE MIC

Years ago when I first got started in business I was asked to do a presentation in front of a group I was part of for one of the local Chambers. Let me tell you, I was terrified.

See, I had come from the music industry and had moved from being a performer to being a stage hand because I had stage fright.

Most of us start out that way. In fact, public speaking is the #1 fear in the world. More so than death itself.

Yes, most people would rather be in the casket than conducting the eulogy.

Today, I'm a speaker and love getting in front of groups. In fact that first presentation I did (while I was shaking, by the way) led to many more speaking opportunities.

They started small with groups of 10 or less and led to groups of as high at 100.

Even a small opportunity to stand up and share with a group is another opportunity to share what you have to offer. Don't think it has to be in groups of hundreds.

Take it one step at a time. Start by leading a small group.

Here are a few places to get started:
- Small leads groups or chambers of commerce
- Lead a group in breakout sessions
- When at a conference, go to the mic and share your experience when given the opportunity.

Start small and over time it will get easier and easier. Just don't skip out on the opportunities all around you.

At one conference I attended there were about 80 people in the room and I was an attendee with everyone else. The host of the event wanted people to come to the mic and share what they got out of the previous session.

I took the opportunity to go to the mic and shared my experience. That one minute on the mic led to me getting swamped with people wanting my card at the next break and having lunch meetings the next 2 days. (It's resulted in $1000's in sales as well).

All because I stood up and talked for 1 minute on the mic.

So, don't think you have to speak on big stages but do remember you need to take advantage of any opportunity you can to share with a crowd. Even a crowd of two.

Networking Tidbit #11

Making A Lasting Impression Starts With One Question...

"What Do You Need?"

NETWORKING TIDBITS #11
MAKING A LASTING IMPRESSION STARTS WITH ONE QUESTION...

Want to make a lasting impression when you first meet someone at any business function? Ask them this one simple question...

"What Do You Need?"

It's amazing how many shocked looks I get when I ask that question.

Think about it, how often do you go to events and have someone genuinely ask about you first? Most of the time it's pretty rare.

Most people are there to tell you everything about their own businesses and forget to even stop to ask if you are looking for something like what they sell.

I've been in conversations (if you can call them that) where someone spent five minutes going on about how awesome they were before even stopping to find out my name.

Sadly enough, it is the norm in most networking environments today. But, it's a great opportunity for you to really stand out.

Simply by asking that one simple question, people are confused.

They're already on the defense waiting for you to go into your pitch and you throw them a curve ball by asking about them and what they need.

You'll immediately stand out and they will remember you.

Of course, you have to be genuine about this. You can't just do this with the goal to "look good". You have to actually be willing to help them.

If they need a landscaper and you know someone, make the introduction. If they need a CPA and you know one that's in the room, walk them over and get them talking.

Trust me on this one, you'll make a much stronger impression than you would by pitching your stuff like everyone else does.

Years ago, I used to run a monthly networking event and it was my goal to stay close to the door and greet everyone who came in.

I'd take them aside and find out more about them and who they were. I'd also ask that one simple question. Almost every person who attended was shocked I'd take the time to really get to know them and ask how I could help them.

Then, to make it even better, I'd take them to someone else at the event I thought would be a good connection for them and introduce the two leaving them to talk and collaborate.

You don't have to start your own events to do this. Just make a point to ask how you can help them before you talk about your own products and services. That conversation will come but show you're there to help them succeed first.

Networking Tidbit #12

"Want To Connect With Someone That You're Not Sure How To Get To, Try LinkedIn."

NETWORKING TIDBITS #12
WANT TO CONNECT WITH SOMEONE YOU'RE NOT SURE HOW TO GET TO, TRY LINKEDIN

LinkedIn is one of the most underutilized social networks out there in my opinion. Funny thing is most of us in business have LinkedIn accounts yet don't actually do much with it.

Now LinkedIn isn't as cool as Facebook or as easy as Twitter but it does truly have some amazing resources.

Want to find people in your industry to connect with, try checking LinkedIn groups and signing up for a few. I believe groups are the most useful part of LinkedIn.

You can see who's in a group, share content and add value to the group and connect with people you think are a good fit for you.

I've connected with people from all over the world via LinkedIn. In fact, I've used it to find guests for my podcast, shared content to drive traffic to my site, and even connected with potential leaders to get speaking gigs.

Start by connecting to people you already know in LinkedIn. See what groups they are part of and, if it's a good fit, start participating in those groups.

Share your thoughts and ideas. Answer questions others might have. Be active in the group and show you're there to help.

Once you've been there for a bit and have built a reputation as someone who wants to give, you can reach out to some of those people you've been wanting to connect with and add them to your network.

That's the door to connecting one-on-one with them.

You might not be able to find their personal email or direct line to call them up, but LinkedIn is one place they are likely paying attention to and will respond to you.

Don't over complicate it and be sure to add value first. You'll make an impression and attract others who will want to know more about you and how you might work together.

Networking Tidbit #13

"Coffee Meetings Can Be Very Powerful As Long As You Plan Ahead"

NETWORKING TIDBITS #13
COFFEE MEETINGS CAN BE VERY POWERFUL AS LONG AS YOU PLAN AHEAD

It's the typical scenario … You're out networking, meeting people and then the question comes up… "*Can we meet for coffee?*"

Coffee meetings can be a double edged sword if you're not careful.

On the plus side, they are one of the best ways to get to know someone and see how you might be able to work with them. Nothing beats one-on-one face time with someone.

But there's a negative side as well.

They can be time consuming and many times it's just a more intimate way for someone to either pick your brain or pitch their wares.

So how do you keep on track and make the most of these meetings?

First off, plan a specific time frame and agenda. If the meeting is set for 30 minutes, then keep to it. I personally like to set them for 45 minutes.

I think that 30 minutes just isn't enough time to really get the juices flowing in a good conversation.

But why 45 minutes?

Because when I line up live meetings, I book them all at the same place back to back. One hour apart to be specific.

See, I know that there will be people who cancel last minute, some will be late and some will need more time, but this keeps me on track and the most effective. I'll take an entire day and book non-stop meetings all day at the same place on one day.

With 45 minutes planned, it gives us a few minutes in case we run long and gives me time between meetings to prep for the next one if needed.

I've had days where I sat in the same spot in a coffee shop for 8 hours.

I'm also very specific in where I meet with people as well. I pick a central location that has food, coffee and WiFi so I can bring my laptop with me.

This way, when someone cancels or no-shows (and some do) I'm not sitting there wasting time. I just pull out my laptop and knock out some writing or reply to a few emails.

It's all about being prepared ahead of time and knowing exactly what to expect for the conversation.

Also, if you're doing more global business, don't forget about Skype for "Virtual Coffee" meetings.

It's the next best thing to a live face to face conversation and no one has to travel anywhere.

I'm known to lock in full days with Skype calls to chat with people all over the globe and see how we can help each other out. As the world gets smaller and smaller, this is becoming much more standard.

Just remember the same rules apply. Plan specific times and set a timer if needed to make sure you stay on track. Have an agenda and be sure to follow up after the call. I like to book a little extra time to shoot off a follow up email immediately after a call I have with someone to recap what we talked about and what the next steps might be.

Coffee meetings, live or virtual, can be a great way to build relationships with potential clients, referral partners or business colleagues. Just be sure to keep on track and plan ahead to make the most of them.

Networking Tidbit #14

"Instead Of Combing Events For Clients, Look For Leverage Partners Who Know 100 Possible Clients"

NETWORKING TIDBITS #14:
QUIT COMBING EVENTS FOR CLIENTS & LOOK FOR LEVERAGE PARTNERS INSTEAD

It amazes me how many people are networking with the hunter mentality. They're on the hunt for the kill. (AKA sell someone something right there)

Several years ago, I figured out one simple shift in my strategy that multiplied my results and simplified my efforts.

Instead of going to events looking for new clients, I go looking for potential leverage partners.

Leverage partners, referral partners, joint venture partners, it doesn't matter what you call them.

These are the people who may not need your products themselves but they serve the same type of clients you do AND have a database of their clients and prospects who might be interested in what you can do to help them.

I like to call them leverage partners because you'll be leveraging each other's assets, lists and relationships. It's about building a win-win-win scenario.

Let's say you find one potential partner who would be willing to cross promote with you. Instead of finding one potential client, you just found someone who may have a list of 100 clients who need your products.

You win - that's 100 new people who get an endorsed exposure to you.

They win - by providing another great resource to help their clients out they look good in the eyes of those clients.

The client wins - they get help in solving a problem they have by you being the knight in shining armor there to help them out.

What's the next business event you plan on going to?

Instead of focusing on finding clients, think about who might be a good leverage partner for you.

What other types of industries also serve the same types of clients that you do?

Write this out before the event.

Now, instead of thinking of direct clients you hope to meet, walk in the door looking specifically for someone who works in the industry you wrote down.

Here's an example:
Let's say you're a computer technician and your clients are small business owners. You might look for a CPA. Not to become a client (which is great as well) but as someone who might be willing to partner up with you to cross promote each other.

Maybe they send an email to their list telling them about a workshop you're having or even sending them an article you wrote about *"The Top 7 Things Most Business Owners Need To Keep Their PCs Running In Top Shape"*.

Of course, you should be willing to do the same for them as well. It may not be in the form of an email as there are a lot of ways to make it a win for everyone. You could give them a referral fee for every client you get because of that email.

This is something I do all the time. I get interviewed for podcasts, write guest blog posts, etc. all the time. Sometimes these are done with affiliate relationships, meaning if I get a client from the promotion, I pay the site owner a commission.

They don't expect me to promote them (though they love that even more) but it does make it a win for them. They get something out of it to make it worth their time.

Leverage partnerships can be as simple as just basic referrals and as advanced as cross promotions in a newsletter, displaying together at a trade show or even putting on workshops together (my favorite).

So, get out there and start looking for leverage partners and see how you can turn one great relationship into 100. All from one person.

Networking Tidbit #15

"The Best Connections Happen After An Event. Plan Ahead By Showing Up Early And Staying Late"

NETWORKING TIDBITS #15
HOW TO GET MORE OUT OF ANY EVENT AFTER IT'S OVER

I hate being late to things. I'm one of those guys who leaves 30 minutes before he really needs to "just in case".

When I first started networking and going to events, I found out pretty early on that this quirk actually worked in my favor.

I'd show up and sometimes get there before the host of the event showed up. Immediately I was able to get a few minutes of time with them to get to know them better and help them set things up.

Instantly, when other people showed up, I looked like I knew what I was doing because I had been there with the host.

Other newbies would walk up to me because I was only one of a few people. It's much easier to talk to a few people than a big group so it was an easy conversation to start.

Over time, I used that ability to meet people as they walked in the door. Instead of walking into a big crowd of people, I was there to meet people one at a time as they walked in the door.

I'm also known to be one of the last people to leave an event. See, many times, the end of an event is when the magic happens.

Nothing solidifies a new relationship like getting together for drinks when everyone is winding down after an event.

You don't even have to drink to join the "after party" group. Just hang out with them and talk shop. I can't count the number of amazing people I've met and really got to know well after the event was over.

See, while the event is going on, everyone is in "presentation mode" and has an agenda for being there. After the event, they let their guard down and are more into real conversation.

Not to mention, many events get really loud and it's hard to have a good conversation with someone. Afterwards, there are less people and the meeting agenda is done.

Side-note: Trade shows are a great example of this. When I've done trade shows, my goal is to network with other vendors more than to talk to the attendees who walk through. I remember my first trade show back when I was promoting my graphic design business.

By staying to the very end and talking to the other vendors as we packed up, I got one client that has been with me to this day. It's over 15 years later.

All because I stuck around for a few extra minutes.

Ely Delaney

Networking Tidbit #16

"Remember When It Comes To Networking You Don't Have To Be In The Same Room To Make A Great Connection"

NETWORKING TIDBITS #16
HOW TO MAKE GREAT CONNECTIONS WITHOUT MEETING IN PERSON

Let's face it, face to face time with someone is and always will be the best way to make a great connection.

Nothing beats being able to look someone in the eye and see the reactions on their face when you have a conversation.

But, this doesn't mean you have to be in the same room to network with people to make great connections.

With the online tools and communities out there I've made some amazing connections with people all over the globe.

Social media is a great way to start a connection with someone who might be a great referral partner, mastermind member, or even a client.

Think about the people who would be great connections for you.

Where do they hang out? Do they spend time on LinkedIn, Facebook, or Twitter? Then connect with them there. Comment on their stuff, ask them questions.

Once you've made a connection and they get to know a bit about you, reach out and see if you can get them on a short call.

With the amazing technology we have today, you can use tools like Skype and Google Hangouts to have a video chat with them.

It's the next best thing to face to face. You still get to see their reactions and it's almost like being in the room.

I've had amazing conversations with other marketers from Australia to London and everything in between (along with all over the US).

These conversations have led to clients in 5 different countries and referral partners all over the globe. All without leaving the comfort of my office.

Networking Tidbit #17

"Make The Most Of Your Next Networking Opportunity By Having A Follow Up Plan BEFORE You Walk In The Door"

NETWORKING TIDBITS #17
HAVE A FOLLOW UP PLAN IN ADVANCE

You've likely heard the phrase...

"The Fortune Is In The Follow Up"

If you're out networking to grow your business, you can't expect to get new business from meeting someone for 5 minutes at an event. The follow up is the key to really getting to know them and making the most of the event.

Yet, so many people have no plan for following up. They wing it most of the time, making a few calls, writing a few emails and usually that's it. (If that much).

If you want to make the most of the next networking event you attend, plan it out now. What EXACTLY is your follow up system?

How do you plan to follow up with them? You might want to write them an email....

So write the basics of the email now.

Imagine you just met someone and you wanted to follow up with them telling them how great it was to meet them. Write the email right now and save it as a text file on your computer. Imagine what you're going to say to them. Chances are, you'd say mostly the same thing no matter who you meet.

"It's was great meeting you at...."

"What other events do you attend?"

"I'd love to get together for coffee sometime next week. What's Thursday look like for you?"

These are things you'd likely say no matter who it was you met. So, write up an email to a "future" connection you meet. Now you have a template ready to start the process after the event.

List exactly what you're going to do after the event to follow up with the people you meet.

Create your "One Page Follow Up Plan" and keep it handy.

Now, after your next event you know exactly what you need to do to make the event a success. Just pull out your plan and start following up.

Networking Tidbit #18

"The Point Of Networking Is NOT To Make A Sale. It's To Build Relationships First."

NETWORKING TIDBITS #18
THE POINT OF NETWORKING IS NOT TO MAKE A SALE

So many times I meet someone at a business event and they go right into how awesome their product is and why I need it.

When I ask someone what they do in their business, I'm looking to get an idea of who they are. Not to listen to a 30 minute infomercial about how awesome they are.

I remember an event I went to a few years ago where I asked a girl what she did and she spend 5 minutes non-stop talking about how they were social media managers and how great they were, all the things they could do for me and how much value I was going to get by using them.

(seriously, it was non-stop. I'm not sure this poor girl even stopped for a breath between sentences.)

Now, I'm all for being enthusiastic about your products and services. I totally get that. I'm known to go into an excited frenzy about things as well.

But... this girl went into full on pitch mode without even asking anything about me. She had no clue if I was interested in what she had to offer.

She hadn't even asked my name or found out what I did to cater her message more to my business.

The funny thing was after her entire pitch, (most of which I was really not interested in and actually quite bored with the fast paced pitch), she finally stopped to ask what I did.

My response... "I teach entrepreneurs how to market their business using the tools they already have access to like social media so they don't have to waste the money to hire a marketing agency that won't give them the results they deserve"

(AKA Pretty much her)

She really didn't know what to say about that. I wasn't trying to be mean to her specifically but I did want to get a point across. She was so into her pre-scripted pitch she forgot to ask the important questions that need to happen in the beginning...

- What's the problem this person has?
- Do my products help them solve it?
- What value can I add to their life right now?

These are the basic questions you need to think about in any first contact with a person. You never know if they are in need of your product or service until you talk to them. You need to know them and their business first.

Then, and only then, do you have enough information to know if your product is the right fit for them.

Most of the time, you don't have time to gather all this in the 5 minutes you get with someone while networking. It takes time.

It takes a conversation in a place with less distractions. It takes building the relationship first.

That's why networking opportunities are best served as "connection" tools.

Walk in the door with the goal to meet people and connect further AFTER the event.

Meet them for coffee. Stop by their office. Even a phone call is a better time to get to know them and their needs.

Networking is to make great connections. Not to pitch your stuff.

Networking Tidbit #19

"If You Are Nervous, Look For A Familiar Face"

NETWORKING TIDBITS #19:
IF YOU'RE NERVOUS, LOOK FOR A FAMILIAR FACE

Have you ever been at an event and just felt a bit freaked out by walking in the door?

Let's face it, even the best of us have off days and can get a little nervous networking in a room.

Maybe you're new to networking or maybe you're a seasoned vet but are in a new room of VIPs.

There have been times where I walked in the room and thought I was going to be ill from the nerves just kicking in.

Me of all people. Me, who loves to network and connect with complete strangers. I've done business with random people in coffee shops before. Yet, I still get nervous in new groups I'm not familiar with.

We all get nervous at one time or another. It's ok.

It's just part of our brain that isn't comfortable with new environments. It's the fight or flight mechanism in our brain trying to take over.

Sometimes it happens just because we're having a bad day.

It doesn't matter what the reason is for it happening. The question is "how do you work through the gut instinct to run?"

The easiest way to overcome this is to look for one familiar face in the room. Just one!

NETWORKING TIDBITS: 25 Ways To Connect, Grow & Succeed Through Networking

Look around and find someone you know already. Even if it's someone you don't know well. It even could be someone you're connected with online. They don't have to be your best friend to help set your mind at ease.

I've been known to walk into a room and only know one person that I met once a year ago. I'll still walk up to them first and re-introduce myself to them.

I instantly feel more comfortable and at ease. It helps me get in the groove.

Just having one face I'm familiar with helps me re-focus and remember why I went to the event in the first place. To meet cool people.

Don't know anyone in the room at all? Try looking for the person who looks the friendliest.

There will always be someone in the room who already knows everyone and THEY are looking to connect with you because they don't know you yet.

That person is likely the best person in the room to connect with anyway. They already know most of the people and will be happy to introduce you to others as well.

Just remember we all get nervous from time to time. Just take a big breath and focus on one person first. Once you connect with them, they can help you get more comfortable with everyone else.

You never know, they might be able to introduce you to your next client.

Networking Tidbit #20

"The Answer To The Question "What Do You Do?" Is Not Your Entire Sales Presentation"

NETWORKING TIDBITS #20:
"WHAT DO YOU DO?" DOESN'T MEAN THEY WANT YOUR LIFE STORY!

We all love our products and are passionate about talking about them, especially when it comes to making a sale, right?

But there is such a thing as WAY too far.

Have you ever been at an event and asked someone what they did and they go into this huge 30 minute pitch about how their product was created using a special plant only found in the back jungles of the Amazon and was handpicked by the aborigines.... (story goes on and on... and on... and on....)

When you first meet someone, they want to know a *bit* about you. It's like the trailer of a movie. You watch it to see if you want to spend another two hours watching it.

Your answer to the question "What do you do?" should be like that trailer. It needs to be impactful, pointed and leave them wanting to spend more time with you.

One way I like to explain what I do is by asking more questions. I turn it back on them and ask them questions like "Well, what are you doing to market your business right now?" That opens up the conversation for me to cater my response to what they are doing and how they might be able to do it better.

That gives me a way to SHOW them what I do versus telling them.

And... they get to talk more about themselves, which in case you didn't know is usually a person's favorite subject.

People love to talk about themselves. They also love to talk about their frustrations and worries. That's human nature. If you can ask the right questions, you'll get them to tell you exactly what problems they have and how they'd like to see them solved.

That's your opportunity to become a trusted adviser for them instead of just another person pitching stuff.

Your goal is to be remembered as that person that was a great listener and had a ton of knowledge to share. If it happens to also involve your company as the source, great!

You just need to ease into it and make sure that the conversation leans that way instead of you pulling them with a noose around their neck.

It's all about keeping their attention. Blasting them with all the facts and figures of your product and how awesome it is won't do that. It will usually scare them off.

So, when someone asks you what you do, ask more questions and be helpful first. It's not an excuse to bring out the flip chart and start a pitch.

Networking Tidbit #21

"After You Meet Someone In Person Continue The Connection On Facebook"

NETWORKING TIDBITS #21
AFTER YOU MEET SOMEONE IN PERSON, CONTINUE THE CONNECTION ON FACEBOOK

Let's say you're at a business event networking with other professionals from anywhere and everywhere. This is usually one of the best ways to make new connections, right?

You meet, you chat and have a great time, and... you do the business card exchange. All the usual stuff.

But, if you REALLY want to connect with them for the long term, reach out to them on Facebook as soon as you can.

You see, Facebook is a social tool that not only allows us to follow up and connect in another media but it also gives us a ton of information about that person.

You can find out more about a person in 5 minutes on their Facebook page than you could in 30 minutes with them face to face.

Think about it. Facebook gives us a place to share who we are, what we're interested in and where we are, all in one place.

After an event, one of the first things I do is connect with someone on Facebook and send them a personal message telling them how great it was to meet them.

I'll even check out their wall and see what types of stuff they talk about. What movies do they watch, what books do they read, what Facebook pages they like, etc.

This gives me a ton of great stuff to talk about with them.

In fact, just a couple of days ago I had someone connect with me that had a photo of her with a couple of the actors from the show Firefly. (It's a Sci-fi geeky thing for anyone that doesn't know the show.)

That gave me something IMMEDIATELY that we could talk about. I'm a fan of the show as well so we have a shared interest (AKA something in common).

What if you're a hockey fan and you realize that someone you connect with is a fan of hockey as well? Doesn't that help make it easier to talk to them? This is all possible!

Facebook is a great way to get to know people and find out what you really have in common other than just buying and selling stuff.

Remember people buy from people they know, like and trust (The famous KLT Factor). You need to get to know them first. They need to get to know you as well if they are going to like you.

Now that you're connected, it's easy to build the relationship even further one small bit at a time by liking and commenting on stuff they post. Even a one sentence response or sharing out something that they post will give you a lot of impact on them.

It makes you stand out and they will take notice of who you are and what you've got to say as well.

Networking Tidbit #22

"Want To Make A Great Impression... Just Smile!"

Ely Delaney

NETWORKING TIDBITS #22
WANT TO MAKE A GREAT IMPRESSION... JUST SMILE!

Seriously, this one shouldn't be a big surprise to you but I couldn't even try to count the number of times I have walked up to someone and they really don't look happy at all.

Let's face it, you don't want to do business with someone who's grumpy.

I know I don't!

It doesn't matter where you are, make a point to smile. Even if you're having a bad day, think about something that makes you happy and put on a smile.

It will make a huge difference on how people react to you and if they are willing to hang out long enough to have a real conversation with you.

I remember a networking group I was part of for many years. We would meet weekly and had breakfast together in a private room at a restaurant.

It never failed I'd end up looking across the table and there was one person that almost always looked mad. She really looked like she didn't want to be there and that she didn't like being there.

Now I knew her well enough to know that wasn't true but the look on her face was what I saw every week.

It was actually draining just to look in her direction. It was no surprise she also did a lot of complaining about not having enough work.

A simple smile would have made all the difference.

Think about when you go out to eat. Do you ever notice when you smile at the server and treat them with respect (instead of slave labor) you get better service?

I do.

I make it my goal to smile and be nice to everyone I interact with as much as I can. I can tell the difference when I do.

And... when I'm talking to a prospect or client I make a point to smile while I'm talking with them. No matter what's going on in the back of my head.

When you smile, you put off the vibe that you're a happy person, maybe even fun. You look like you love what you're doing (passionate about your business) and that you are enjoying the conversation with them.

By the way, even when you're on the phone you need to smile as well. They can't see you but smiling changes the tone of your voice and they can hear the difference. When you are talking to a prospect or client, stand up while you're talking and be sure to smile like you're standing right in front of them. Your energy level will rise and they will feel the difference.

So, make a point to stop and smile more. It's great for you personally and will make a huge difference in how people see you and their desire to hang out with you.

Yes... it is that simple!

Networking Tidbit #23

"Want To Really Get To Know Someone? Ask A Lot Of Questions!"

NETWORKING TIDBITS #23
WANT TO REALLY GET TO KNOW SOMEONE? ASK A LOT OF QUESTIONS!

People want to know you actually care about them. That's what's important to them.

When we're out networking, we want people to be interested in who we are and what we're there for. Usually, our businesses are something we're really excited about and we want to share it with the world.

So, if you want to make a lasting impression on someone, ask a lot of questions about them and their business. Truly get to know them and what they are all about.

I know it amazes me even to this day when I get talking to someone and they start asking a lot of questions. It makes it easy for me to talk about my stuff and since it's something I'm passionate about I really can get on a roll.

What happens because of this?

I have an energized feeling about that person. They really listened to me and cared about my business and what I have to offer.

They stand out much better than the person who doesn't seem to care about anything I say. (we've all ran into them as well)

If you want to make a huge impression on someone, ask them questions and truly be interested in them.

How long have you been in the business?
What got you into this industry?

What types of clients do you love working with?
etc.

These are all the types of questions you can ask to really get them going and find out who they REALLY are. That's a great part about this. By asking questions like this, the person you're talking to will start to let their guard down and you can really have a good conversation.

Think about it, how often does someone walk up to you and you think "What's this guy going to pitch me?"

I know I'm guilty of this and you may be too. It's ok, because we're used to getting bombarded by people at networking events pitching us on how awesome their stuff is without even stopping to ask our names.

By taking the time to stop and ask questions, you're opening it up for others to be authentic.

By the way, by asking a lot of questions, you're opening up to learn a lot about them and find out where they will fit into your network.

Maybe they are a great prospect for you.
Maybe they would be a perfect referral source.
Maybe you can send them some clients as well.
Maybe they are a connector who happens to know the right type of person you're needing to connect with.

You'll never know without asking the right questions first.

Ely Delaney

Networking Tidbit #24

"Networking Is A Long Term Skill. Don't Expect To Be A Master Your First Time Out."

NETWORKING TIDBITS #24
NETWORKING IS A LONG TERM SKILL. DON'T EXPECT TO BE A MASTER YOUR FIRST TIME OUT

I can't count how many times I've heard people say "networking doesn't work. It's just a waste of time."

Well, I'm here to tell you networking does work. It takes time and it takes skill to get it to work, but when it does, it can easily become your most powerful marketing tool.

First off, remember that networking is about relationships. Don't expect to walk into a room of strangers and walk out with a hand full of sales.

You're there to meet and connect with people. In all my years, I've only walked into an event once and walked out with cash in hand for one of my workshops.

Rarely will you ever find a sale right there at the event your first time out.

Most of the time it's going to take some follow up. You need to build enough rapport at the event to get them intrigued and interested enough to follow up with a call, meeting, etc.

That's why you need to make following up after the event your number one priority to see your numbers multiply.

People buy from people they know, like and trust. You've heard that before. (Maybe even from me.) Remember it takes time for people to start trusting you.

I had one group I went to every week for 6 months before I got my first real sale.

Then, the ice was broken and I ended up getting over 80% of the members as clients. Some are still clients to this day. (18+ years later)

It takes time for others to see you're serious and professional. They don't want to trust their business to a fly-by-night organization. Over the years it's still amazed me how many people I see show up to an event once or twice and then get upset because they didn't get any business.

You need to give people time to trust you. Even if it's via email, phone calls, and coffee meetings after the event, etc.

You've got to stick around to give them a chance to see you're legit.

Networking is also a trial by fire type of marketing. You don't know if an event or group will be a good fit until you test it out. I've been to events I was sure would be perfect and found out after the fact that they were just not the right fit for me.

On the other hand, I've been to groups I didn't expect much from that ended up bringing in a bunch of sales, referrals and long term clients I love to work with.

You never know until you give it a true chance.

As you're out there more, you'll get better at picking the right places to network and find the prospects, referral partners and connectors who are a great fit for you and where you want to go with your business.

It takes some time and effort but stick with it. You'll get better and see massive results by looking at the long term, not the short one.

Networking Tidbit #25

"What's The One Thing People Love To Talk About The Most? Themselves! So Let Them And You'll Make An Impact They Will Never Forget."

NETWORKING TIDBITS #25
PEOPLE LOVE TALKING ABOUT THEMSELVES. SO LET THEM!

Let's face it, we're all a little egocentric to one degree or another.

We love talking about ourselves, our families, our pets, our businesses, etc. That's the stuff that's most important in our world. Therefore, we love talking about them.

When you're out networking, the fastest way to make a great impression on someone is to let them talk about the stuff THEY love to talk about most.

It puts you instantly in a position of being a "great listener" (which, by the way is a trait people love about others).

You become the person who was super helpful and really listened to them. The best part about this is all this information they talk about gives you more insight to how they think and what's important to them.

What better way to get research about someone than to get it directly from them telling you? I love to think of this as research into how I can cater the conversation moving forward.

By doing this, you can shift how you talk to them and what you say based on their personality.

One of the best things I've ever done is let someone talk about their business, how long they've been in business, why they do what they do, etc. and then when they ask what I do, I can cater the message to talk about terms they get. Things they already are interested in.

They are much more likely to get what I do if I can talk about it in terms they will understand. You talk their language.

You can't do that if you don't know much about them to begin with.

Think about the last time you met someone in a conference or other business event. Was the conversation amazing or was it boring?

If it was amazing, think back and see if you were the one doing most of the talking. Chances are you were.

That's exactly the same feeling others have when they get to talk about themselves and their businesses. The great thing about this is you'll be the one who gave them that great conversation... even if the hardest part of the entire conversation for you was to not say anything.
:)

RESOURCES

Throughout this book there are various sites, tools and resources mentioned.

We have pulled them all together and listed them all in one easy place for you.

To find them all in one place please go here:
http://YMUBooks.com/nt01resources

ABOUT THE AUTHOR

Ely Delaney

Ely Delaney is the co-founder of Your Marketing University, the host of the Driving Your Marketing podcast and a Bestselling Author. Almost two decades ago he discovered that while his clients loved him, he was going to need more than 2 of them to pay the bills. After a trip to the book store to pick up a book on how to market that company, a lifelong obsession with marketing education was born.

His collection of books, conference notes and training videos on marketing would rival any University library in the country and he is always looking for more to learn. Ely is passionate about helping people bring their dreams of business success to life and spends every waking moment focused on that goal. He believes all entrepreneurs have greatness inside of them, they just need the right marketing to let the world know.

Today, having trained hundreds of entrepreneurs and professionals all around the globe, Ely has been a speaker and trainer for groups such as S.C.O.R.E., David Fagan's Icon Builder Bootcamp, National Association Of Women Business Owners, Arizona Small Business Association, Chambers of Commerce, American Business Women's Conference and many more. He is determined to help entrepreneurs take control of their marketing by removing their fear and showing them the step by step way to make it happen.

CONNECT WITH ELY ONLINE

On Facebook: http://facebook.com/elydelaney

On Twitter: http://twitter.com/elydelaney

On LinkedIn: http://linkedin.com/in/elydelaney

On Google Plus: https://plus.google.com/+ElyDelaney

On Instagram: http://instagram.com/elydelaney

Upcoming Events: http://meetup.com/ymurocks

ABOUT MARKETING TIDBITS

Marketing Tidbits: 50 Quick & Easy Ways To Grow Your Business

"But isn't marketing hard and expensive?"

It's a question that's all too common. The common myth for most budding entrepreneurs is that marketing is about having big budgets and billboards.

If you're in business and are running in a thousand directions to get things rolling, this book is just for you. Every marketing tidbit in this book is designed to keep it simple and show you that marketing is in everything we do.

It's not an event, it's a way of life and we're all doing it anyway. Let's do it the right way and keep things simple.

Available in Paperback & Digital

http://ymubooks.com

www.ingramcontent.com/pod-product-compliance
Lightning Source LLC
Chambersburg PA
CBHW072036190526
45165CB00017B/950